Animal Magnetism

poems by

Colleen Wells

Finishing Line Press
Georgetown, Kentucky

Animal Magnetism

For Jim, who also never gives up

It is so wonderful to watch an animal
because an animal has no opinion of itself.
Eckert Tolle

Copyright © 2022 by Colleen Wells
ISBN 978-1-64662-843-8 First Edition
All rights reserved under International and Pan-American Copyright Conventions. No part of this book may be reproduced in any manner whatsoever without written permission from the publisher, except in the case of brief quotations embodied in critical articles and reviews.

ACKNOWLEDGMENTS

"Watching," "A Bug's Life," "Second Hand Smoke," "What is the Lesson?" and "Seedlings," have previously published by *The Voices Project*
"Caterpillar Cue" appeared in *New Southerner* 2006
"The Hawk" was a runner-up for the Robert Frost Poetry Foundation Award 2020
Versions of "Rascal," "Summertime and the Livin' is Almost Easy," "Small Zoo," "Freedom," and "My Corner of the Universe," were included in *Dinner with Doppelgangers—A True Story of Madness & Recovery* Wordpool Press (2015)
A version of "My Corner of the Universe" appeared in *Ravensperch*
"Birth and Death in a Microcosm" was published by *Bohemian Pupil* July 2014

Publisher: Leah Huete de Maines
Editor: Christen Kincaid
Cover Art: Dorothy Sabean
Author Photo: Rick Wells
Cover Design: Elizabeth Maines McCleavy

Order online: www.finishinglinepress.com
also available on amazon.com

Author inquiries and mail orders:
Finishing Line Press
PO Box 1626
Georgetown, Kentucky 40324
USA

Table of Contents

Watching 1
High-flying Bird 2
Summertime and the Livin' Is Almost Easy 3
Rascal 5
Small Zoo 6
Freedom 7
A Bug's Life 8
Roadkill 9
Second Hand Smoke 10
Caterpillar Cue 11
Easter in the Park with a Doe 12
Angelbee Funeral 14
Ode to a Yellow Finch 15
Seedlings 16
What is the Lesson? 17
Here Today, Gone Tomorrow 18
Plugged In 20
Clarion Call 22
Autumnal 23
The Hawk 24
Water 25
My Corner of the Universe 26
Dog Tired 29
Soulspeak 31
Full-circle 32
Gardening with the Aunts 33
Birth and Death in a Microcosm 34

"Watching"

Woods and water sheltered me as a child in
my tiny corner of the world.
In the woods I could hide under a fortress of vines
or crawl down a ravine.
I could hear the crunching of leaves under my feet
or smell the sweet musk of wet earth.
I could find a caterpillar on the back of a green leaf.

I let him be.
And he became something beautiful that I never saw.

Across the gravel road, I could step into the glossy-clear lake and
press my toes into sand
and shells and rocks.
I could twirl around, slicing my hands through the water
as schools of minnows darted back and forth like a collective soul.
I could float or merely sit by the shore and think vast thoughts
or think nothing at all.

But sometimes a chilly air would come, and a rushing wind bent
the blades of grass.
My siblings and I would have to come in during storms even
though we didn't want to.
Through the screened porch we watched lightning smack down
illuminating the sky like a signal to pay attention.
The wind whipped up the water making foamy waves and the lake
became a black sea.

And we watched.
We watched it be.

"High-flying Bird"

Lamb's wool. Cotton candy,
cotton balls, sea turtles.
Angels and Elmer Fudd.
A polar bear and Zoom!
A high-flying bird zips through them
ripping through my
cloudstudy.

"Summertime and the Livin' Is Almost Easy"

In the summers we go to the lake cottage for long periods of time.
We are only allowed to pack one paper grocery sack each
for our clothes;
and I'm to pack layers, so my hooded sweatshirt goes on the bottom,
then jeans and long-sleeved shirts, then shorts and t-shirts
plus a skirt for church.
I have to keep mashing it down and being careful not to tear the bag.
My toothbrush and paste and hair bands go in a
sandwich baggie on top.

Then once the bags are all in the back of the big blue van, we pile in
and get in our assigned seats.
I'm not allowed to talk too much during the drive,
because my stepdad doesn't like it,
so if I talk too much, then I have to be quiet for four minutes.

Those four minutes seem to last forever.
When I can't take not being allowed to talk any more,
I pretend my fingers are people and tell them the things in my head.
I tell them we have to be quiet for four minutes or I'll get moved to
the back.

At the lake when our chores are done, I sit by the water and read
under big, old trees
whose roots are never thirsty, cuz' they're so close to water.
My friends are the characters in my books:
Runaway Ralph, Ramona and Beezus, Amelia Bedelia,
Charlie Bucket, and Nancy Drew, depending on my age.

During the night when our parents take the boat to see friends,
we sneak bread slathered in sugar and cinnamon.
My brother climbs the rafters like a stealthy cat,
and the older kids tell me ghost stories outside in the dark.
Their voices get real low and serious to make them spookier.

Someone is always on the lookout for the
glowing lights of the deck boat,
and for awhile I feel like I'm part of something,
even though some of the stories are too scary; like
the one they told me about the couple on a date at night in the park.

They said the couple kept hearing a noise, something scraping against
the car roof.
The boy said it's just a twig, but the girl wasn't so sure.
Finally the boy got out and looked and it was
a man hanging from a tree.
The noise was from his toenails scratching on top of the car
as he tried to get in.

Suddenly we saw the tell-tale orange of the boat and scattered to our
bunk-beds, because we knew we'd get in trouble for still being up.
My heart thumped as I got in fake sleep mode.

My heart hoped our parents would go out again soon
so they would tell me the rest of the story.

"Rascal"

Today I see a dead raccoon in the road.
It wears a grimace and has a rib poking up
  through its belly.
It makes me think how when I was a kid
we had a tame, orphaned baby raccoon named Rascal.

Mom gave him rides on the tractor.
Once, after a ride, my mom set him down, so she could finish,
but he ran back for more.
Then instead of reaching for her, he got distracted by the shiny
rotating blade;
  before Mom could cut the engine, his little hands
reached for it instead.

"Small Zoo"

I have a small zoo in my room—
an ant farm, gerbils, goldfish, and sea-monkeys.
After my gerbils, who are thought to both be males, have babies,
I awake one morning to discover that the heads of the tiny creatures
had been chewed off—probably by the mother.

I scream for my parents. My stepdad takes care of the carnage
while I am at school. I told him to take the gerbil parents back to the
pet store too.
When I come home from school, the whole cage is gone
along with evidence of the demise of half
a dozen gerbil children.

"Freedom"

Annie's favorite thing, besides riding shotgun,
is running wild through the woods
at Lake Griffy. The second I unclamp her leash,
she takes off with the speed of a Greyhound.

I follow her into the woods,
hear her feet thumping down the path
                        as she disappears.
In moments like this, we are both free.

"A Bug's Life"

On a trip to North Carolina, one of the largest dragonflies I have ever seen smacks our windshield. It is like a tiny helicopter coming in for a crash landing. The impact tears its enormous wings, giving them the jagged crosshatch design of a broken porch screen.

I watch the dragonfly's legs move slightly and wonder if it was the wind or the last evidence of life. Rick turns on the wipers, but the insect stays wedged between the windshield and the right wiper for the remainder of the trip. Rick keeps saying, "Don't look at it." Our sons are oblivious, sitting in the back playing with their Game Boys.

When we get to Wilmington, our destination, I ask Rick to pull into a subdivision, where I slowly pluck the insect from the windshield, half-hoping it is still alive, vainly wishing that it survived not only the crash, but also the two-hour trip at 70 mph.

I lay the dead dragonfly in the yard and examine it. The coloring is a gorgeous dark metallic green— a color I've seen before on fancy cars.

His legs curl in finality. My husband interrupts me, calling out the window, "Come on, you're embarrassing me."

"Roadkill"

We're bearing down on the Sunshine State.
Quite a road trip from Indiana.
While the speed-limit along I-95 is 70mph,
most people are doing 80-90 mph.
The sides of the road are littered with trash, blown tires and roadkill.
We cross a small body of water called Turtle Creek.
Before we even get to the mouth of the bridge, I see dead turtles
strewn all over the road.
There are cracked armadillo shells too.
The shards are almost pretty to look at like shells at the beach.

Soon afterward, I note a dead Pit-bull surrounded by vultures.
Rick slows down.
We exchange glances; he looks especially sad.
Lowering his voice so the boys can't hear, he tells me
the dog's eyes were gone.

"Second-hand Smoke"

Mama Cardinal, your nest tucked in the tree,
poking against our porch like a big ole' belly in a too-tight shirt,
is woven so perfect.
It's as finely done as the crown on Jesus' head.

You've been fussing over your two blue eggs
speckled with brown spots, little potato eyes.
Mama Cardinal,
you are nature and,
you are nurture.

It's so smart the way you wove your nest right here,
where it's shielded
from rain
   and hawks.

Daddy Cardinal got on board today, Mama,
fed you a fat worm,
so you didn't have to worry and wonder
about whether to leave em' or feed em'.

Mama Cardinal, warming your chicks way up high,
if I don't quit smoking here
while I sit beside you, watching,
we all gonna' die.

"The Caterpillar Cue"

While riding shotgun in the van with the window open
a butterfly bounces off the roof and lands on my leg,
leaving a trail of pale yellow mucus.

I squirm at the sight, and pick up the dead insect.
In the split second I hold it before flinging
it out the window, I notice its brown and orange wings
are warm and soft like velvet.

I feel rattled by its death, plus stress.
In addition to getting acclimated, I have yet to find a job,
we are doing some remodeling,
and the kids will be starting school soon.
I sigh, so much to do.

Later that day at the local art center
I notice a painting of a butterfly,
its wings unfolding in a spray of colors.
I realize I've seen more butterflies during those first weeks
in Aiken then I've seen in my whole life.

Some are as big as birds.
I'd see them on flowers,
or flitting above my head by our swimming pool,
or bobbing in the tall grass alongside the road.
I'd watch them dart across the yard, eluding Maggie, our golden-
retriever mix.

It seems the butterflies are appearing in full force
reminding me of the possibility
of a graceful transition.

"Easter in the Park with a Doe"

Brach's gives to Easter jellybeans
Russell Stover, truffles.
The neighborhood moms tuck
pastel colored M&M's, hollow milk chocolate bunnies,
and yellow marshmallow ducklings dressed in shiny foil
 into dozens of plastic eggs.
But it's the dollar bills the kids want the most.

Clad in Nike athletic-wear, the mothers scurry about
scouting for trees or bushes in the neighborhood park,
but there is not enough foliage to hide all of the eggs.
They will have something to say to the homeowner's association
about this.

A doe lolls by nonplussed.
She stops, nibbles on some edging of a yard, then sashays over to
inspect a hosta.
Her head rises; the beast glances around wary, yet regal
despite the tracking system tethered from her neck.
The device is bigger than most cell phones but not quite the size of an
iPad mini.

A mom extracts her cell phone.
She checks the time then logs into Facebook.
Next she plucks a hot pink plastic egg from her reusable grocery bag,
fills it with a snack-sized bag of Skittles.
It makes a little poppy puff of air noise as it opens.

When she finishes, she prepares to document the feat with a selfie,
planting her legs in a confident stance.
If she were in her Monday morning yoga class, the pose could be
called Easter Egg Hunt Warrior.

The woman raises the phone above her head,
  maneuvers the camera away from the sunlight,
  smiles grandly, and snaps the pic,
her brain giddy thinking of how many likes
the image will net her.

The doe darts across the street,
  spooked.

"Angelbee Funeral"

Shrouded in dust, stymied coal eyes,
  gold and onyx-lined abdomen,
a decorated sentinel.

Wings draped behind its head
like the Christmas angels
plucked from plastic totes
in the attic.
Their lacy gowns littered
with mouse droppings.

I hover over the bee with my broom,
make a clean sweep.
Don't look in the dustpan;
it has been gone for some time.

"Ode to a Yellow Finch"

Your upbeat yellow feathers
and handsome black markings
shock my eyes.

You are a beefy finch.

Claws turned inward
like I curl my toes for a good stretch.
Head covered by fallen oak leaves.

What mishap happened here?

"Seedlings"

She tucked the seeds into the cool dirt,
covering them like a secret.
Later, she watered them, feeling hopeful.

She watched over them each day, still wishing.
When she thought she could wait no more,
tiny shoots pushed from the dirt,
new and bright green like obvious metaphors.

They grew, reaching toward the sun
until they flowered.
She praised them,
and rejoiced.

She did her best to keep them from drying out,
or choking from weeds.
She hoped no pests could destroy them,
and watched intently for signs of disease.

They grew tall and full of color, the brightest red
and richest purple she had ever seen.
She celebrated like a pep band trumpet,
bleating proud.

And when they began to wither and brown,
scattering their leaves in the wind,
she knew she could do nothing more for them
but wait, and wish for their return.

That's all she could do.

"What is the Lesson?"

My newborn niece, Marissa, died yesterday. Word came while attending a protest of the planned deer kill at a nature preserve called Lake Griffy on the north side.
As I think about my sister's loss, I've got the bond between mother and child on the brain.

I spoke to Marge Davis, a 94-year-old wildlife rehabilitator in Sonoma, California, whom I'd found while doing research for my story about the widely-debated kill. I wanted to know more about the bond between does and fawns, as many of those bonds would break if the sharpshooters conduct the kill.

Marge explained that fawns are with their mothers
for nearly two years.
During this time they are taught to find nutritious
food and water sources
and how to avoid predators.

These are also some of the same basic things human mothers teach their children.

Marge said when a doe dies, her fawns will stay by her body circling around as long as she is there. Conversely, she has seen does follow her truck for hundreds of yards when she carries off an injured fawn.

While juvenile fawns in the Griffy area can survive the loss of their mothers, they will be at greater risk, as they won't even yet be yearlings.
We all have a finite amount of time to teach our children, and I ask, what is the lesson in this?

"Here Today, Gone Tomorrow"

Bears, Bears
brown, black, polar white like the whooshing blinding snow
that is almost gone.
The bears too, they, are almost done.

Grizzly bear paws cut for ashtrays
to display on your ivory table.
Snub your smoke into his palms,
he could wipe out your eyes with one claw.

Black bears in Asia
killed for gall bladders
Pestle and mortar.
Ancient medicine, ancient Money.

Bears changing range
moving north,
searching for their northernmost
  Star
so they can breathe, eat, mate.

Bears displayed behind cold steel
where lions and tigers already weep
and gorillas draw sad faces
  in their own shit.

Here today, gone tomorrow.

In Churchill, Manitoba,
polar bears lumber through during migration.
They walk in silence,
hungry,
owning the town.

No one locks up their houses
so they can scramble straight into the nearest home,
even barricade the door
  if they're quick enough—

Light's out!

Artwork by Dorothy Sabean

"Plugged In"

Technology makes you fast
and slow at the same time.
Time disappears and
memory fades
like the sad drone of a trumpet.
Technology makes you high
and low at the same time.
Depends on how many likes and if you have enough bytes.
Meanwhile radiation bounces off your frontal lobe and leaks into your
ear,
pings off the metal in your underwire bra, kills sperm,
dumbs down your baby cousin.

No matter.
It's time to upgrade again
and update again.
This version will be snappy
and shiny
and quick and sleek
and flashier
and it will be dope and you can put likes on likes and now with so many
options for emojis you no longer need
  emotions.

Where did those feelings go?
Don't worry, your cell phone can help locate them.
It knows what you need,
listens to you. Won't nag you about   your
  dwindling
              attention
    span

When the time comes to replace your phone, because the old one
would only net sixty on eBay;
you toss it, watching as it lands in a goo of egg yolk
and wet newspaper.
In the landfill your outdated device bleeds cadmium into the earth
creating an intricate web of chemical poison;
bromine pollutes broccoli,
benzene laces burgers, mercury spikes milk.

That doesn't matter—can't worry about chemicals when you
gotta check your Twitter feed, your Story, upload another selfie to
Instagram; you'll get to Facebook later,
because that's for the grandparents anyway.
Plus, you gotta see if you got new texts from anyone
in the last ten seconds,
because you forgot to take your phone into the bathroom again.

This is actually a good thing because
did you know one in six cell phones has fecal matter on it?
A Google search said so. Therefore, it must be true.
That right there proves technology has the capability to create a lot of
shit.

Feel free to Like, Share, Retweet, or
unfriend me.

"Clarion Call"

The stars know it,
  the moon does too.
Polar bears know it
  and protozoa, too.

The bees are dying
  by the swarm.
The snow is almost gone,
  the monarchs and
tree frogs too,

You know
  it's just a matter of time
  before it's me,
and it's
  you.

"Autumnal"

Autumn is thirsty this year.
The leaves are slow to turn,
haven't seen any burning candy apple reds
or oranges like clementines
with a touch of sass.

No crisp crunch in the air
greeting my face with surprise,
filling my lungs with clean dry oxygen
that cools my chest and calms my soul.

Instead there is only muggy drizzle,
oppressive heat.
Two showers a day it takes
to rid the smudge.

What will we do to get clean
when water becomes scarce?
A commodity, perhaps the last resource
the earth will give
before everything runs dry

including the linings
in the pockets
 of thieves.

"The Hawk"

Serene, white-faced warrior, wise as an owl,
but with a craftiness all its own.
In a neighbor's yard, planted on the branch of an oak tree,
the hawk worked over
its lifeless prey, busy as a chicken scratching in the dirt for a bug.

We stopped walking, took it in. My husband was entranced with it all.
"It looks like he got a mole," he said with satisfaction.
He hates the moles in our yard;
we've argued more than once about his wish to eradicate them with
lethal means.

Just then the giant bird grabbed up the flaccid rodent, clutched it in
its talons, then swooped, black wings flapping like a magician waving
his cape. He landed in another nearby tree,
to feast unfettered by us,
is my guess.

We took a few steps, admiring him again.
"I don't really want to watch this." I said.
My husband commented the hawk was about the same size as our
Jack Russell.
"He can't be that big," I disagreed.
"Can't you see Kramer up in the tree? At that far away,
he'd look the same."

I thought to myself, *Maybe without his four legs, maybe just his head
and chest would equal the size of the hawk.*
But I agreed with my husband.
I looked up at the killer who held me in its vacant amber eyes for a
powerful split second.

"Pretty Bird. You are a pretty bird," I said, unable to stop myself from
saying it.

"Water"

If I could live on water,
what would life be like?
Would my days be better if I could awake
to gaze at a lake or an ocean,
smile at its calm pull,
 mysterious and moody?

Do I love water because
I can't see what's below the surface?
Is it because it seems strong,
impervious to outside forces?

Is it the blue and green colors
I like so well?
Or the way sunshine reflects off the top,
translucent like fish scales?

Water has its sea nymphs and secrets,
sunken pirate ships and war vessels,
mermaids and sharks.

It is expansive;
ripples growing
wider,

 even as we shrink.

"My Corner of the Universe"

Wind rustles through trees sounding like hula skirts. A blue cotton candy sky pops above the evergreens forming a fortress at the back of our yard. Near where I sit on our porch, a giant old oak and shiny magnolia tree offer additional privacy, their limbs reaching out to each other as if beckoning for a hug. The crepe myrtles buffer us from the neighbors, dripping shocks of white and fuchsia blooms. A black faux-wrought-iron fence encases the area, extending enough to give the dogs room to run, but not at full speed.

This morning in my corner of the universe choruses of insect and bird chirps swell the air. My radio plays light jazz. Dude, our Jack Russell, sleeps in a patch of sun on the wooden planks near my feet. Shadows from the trees form lattice-work on the grass. The porch floor sits four feet above the ground. Below me are hostas, monkey grass and rose bushes. They are encroaching on one another, siblings fighting for attention. A yellow tiger swallowtail flits around the plantings, bobbing about, without alighting on anything like it's got too many options.

This sanctuary has not always been so serene. It was a prison when Rick locked the fence gate, his attempt to keep me at home during a long bout of mania. I paced, listening for the airplanes overhead while plotting my escape. I was sure they were full of people I knew, coming to rescue me. "Rescue" was a theme in my ping-ponging thoughts. I believed a former professor was living in my son's closet, waiting to save me. When my aunt came to help, I gave her tokens for him believing she also knew of his location upstairs. One time I pressed a red bandanna into her hands. "You know who to give this to," I instructed.

I don't know the exact moment when I turned the corner into madness. Perhaps it was when I heard larger-than-life bird song or spied John the Baptist and other Biblical figures at the end of our cul-de-sac. Next I became convinced the Obamas had moved in across the street, and prepared a welcome basket for them. When we ordered pizza one night I told our sons there was poison in the Sierra Mist.

Rick and my aunt decided they could no longer keep me safe at home, so I was hospitalized. There a new sanctuary awaited me consisting of a round table in the corner of the day room where I colored, listened to music, and wrote letters to everyone I could think of including that professor. But this wasn't the same as our back porch at home. Other patients crowded me to assess my drawings or have someone to cry next to. Instead of insect chatter or the hum of wind, there was just the chronic drone of institutional lighting and stale air punctuated by the occasional crackle of speakers igniting sharp demands for assistance when a patient needed to be restrained or was having a seizure.

As the days wore on, my paranoia abated, but by then I believed the tapioca pudding offered after evening group was something to look forward to. And then the pendulum in my brain swung. Fatigue, indifference to food, waking up early feeling as though I'd wept in my sleep were all signs I was slipping into depression. My new, quiet way convinced the doctors and staff I was well enough to be discharged. When I walked outside for the first time, the parking lot looked huge like it might swallow me. I blinked, trying to adjust my eyes to the gift of sunlight.

Once home I sat on the back porch, waiting for happy.
But happy didn't come.
Instead, I sank further, slumping in porch furniture staring blankly or sleeping for hours. When I reached out to friends on the phone, I had nothing to say, but took a small comfort in knowing they were on the other end.

The tinkering of psychotropic medication jolted my system, causing side effects like my hair to start falling out. I was also passing dark, amber-colored urine. It took several attempts with different meds and varying dosages to lift the heavy black veil of despair. And even with that, my sadness lingered for several weeks, fading only with time, like a bruise.

Rick and I sit out back in the evenings. We like it when it is breezy and cool. Strings of lights crisscross the ceiling, casting a comforting glow. A cherub knick-knack rests her chubby face on a book seeming to protect the words within, or maybe she is protecting me.

I listen for sounds of our sons cutting through the yard on their way home from playing.
They are starting to trust that it's the real me waiting for them at home.

· · ·

The trees in the wind seem to whisper, "Hush, hush." I do not mention the imprisonment or hospitalization, nor does Rick. Instead, we talk about our sons, the dogs, his job, my writing. We study wildlife always hoping to see a Carolina bluebird. We wait for butterflies as if they are sacred promises.

I hardly ever notice the drone of airplanes, circling above.

"Dog Tired"

Give me your tired old bones
 your gnarled hips jutting out
like crescent moons
 and I will warm them.

Give me your sore joints
 and stiff muscles.
I will take the edge off
 with supplements and laser therapy
 when I can afford it.

Give me your failing eyes,
murky amber stones
shrouded in white fur
 and I will lead you outside.

Give me your deaf ears,
 and I will teach you more sign language.
You already know when I
 beckon you with my hand, it means,
"Here girl, come on. Let's go out for a walk."

I will be your constant protector,
 as you've been mine.
And if you get too tired
 of all of it—those aches and pains,
those small, arduous steps
the deformed bones,
 those cloudy eyes,
and silent ears…

I hate it, but I love you
  and I'll let you go, Maggie.
I'll say goodbye
  to my very best girl,

and I will give you rest,
and you,
you will shoot up beyond
the stars.

"Soulspeak"

In nature I can listen
to wind rustle through
the leaves,
birdsong and crickets.
The chatter in my mind
quiets,
so my soul can speak.

"Full-circle"

From the porch I watched the rain
form a puddle in the driveway;
perfect circles gathered within its borders,
each created by a quiet droplet.

How long had it been
since I watched
a sublime gift like this?
Too long, I say.

I marveled at the pattern.
It reminded me of a painting
I'd done as a kid.
It was of circles, painted in thick globs of red and yellow.
These water circles were as clear as a glacial lake.

I zipped up my coat all the way.
It was getting cold,
but I stayed and watched
the geometric wonder.

"Gardening with the Aunts"

I was picking up sticks,
When I saw a northern map turtle lying near a tree;
I let it be.

Later I told my aunt Sue,
and she said she saw it too,
yesterday, and that she let it be.
I did the math realizing this meant it was very likely dead.

I soon afterward showed aunt Jane
who confirmed it was dead with a tap of her rake.
"That's the part of nature I hate," she said.
"I wonder what happened to it," I mused. "Where did it go?"
"It died," she said.
"But is the turtle still inside?" I asked.
"No. It's just a shell," she said, flipping it over,
exposing the pale-yellow plastron.
It shocked my eyes like neon.

I stood, puzzled,
then realized I'd had this exact conversation
with an older adult as a child.
"We'll give it a proper burial later," my aunt promised,
as if that would fix things.

We got busy,
and never did.

"Birth and Death in a Microcosm"

Our screened-in porch is a cavernous space with a large wooden table and chairs.
Lights are strung haphazardly around the perimeter. Candle-holding fixtures and wind-chimes hang randomly on hooks left by the previous home-owner. In one corner sits a pile of wood for fires we rarely make. In another, a grill we only sometimes use. The bead-board ceiling is a burnt red. My hand-painted birdhouses boast more whimsical colors like lime-green, teal, and lavender. Embellished with lost buttons, lids from bottles of Heineken, and beach glass, they sit on the ledge below the screen.

A small tree abuts the middle of the longest wall. Pressing against the screen, it holds an abandoned bird's nest wedged in its branches. The cardinal pair who inhabited it recently fed their three hungry babies. My husband and I cheered them on, then one evening we noticed only two were raising their little heads to eat worms; we hope the third chick didn't perish because of our dogs.

Birth and death occurring in a microcosm.

I take a sip of my now stale and cooling coffee, noting stuff piled and strewn on the slatted table in front of me. Mounds of books about writing, magazines, journals, notes from the kids' schools and file folders filled with submission guidelines and looming deadlines surround my spot. My family is occupied, so I'm feeling both grateful and guilty about this alone time. While I sit, insects chatter.

Even though it's humid, I can no longer smell the acrid, musky scent of dog urine entrenched in the wooden planks of the floor. We put our incontinent, blind and deaf Rat Terrier down last Monday. He had always been without sight, but when he lost his hearing he began circling.

He'd circle fast, too, to the point I wondered if he was
slowly going insane.
The vet could not find a biological cause for his behavior.

Rusty had always been a regal beast, holding his head high. But the
circling was causing him to lose weight. Not having the ability to
hear his unseen world proved too much, and yet he'd seem to go
round and round with purpose, sometimes until he stumbled. As
he declined and continued to circle, I wondered if it was his way of
attempting suicide.

A small table I am restoring sits at the opposite end of my workspace.
It is only half-way painted. Like everything else, it begs for attention.
I hear the sound of claws on glass, then the swoosh as Louie, our
young, Rottweiler-Shepherd mix pushes the sliding doors open. He
scampers over, nudges his nose into the crook of my arm.

At almost two he is still full of puppy. Because he is a large dog,
it is unlikely he will live as long as Rusty did. Louie's exuberance
reminds me that life is fleeting, but full. As I pet him the swell of birds
chirping to one another from the oak and sycamore trees
        fills the air.

Colleen Wells believes writing can be a wonderful tool for healing, experiencing joy, and connecting people together to share their lives' stories.

She is the editor of Wordpool Press, and has acted as editor for *One in Four*, a collection of narratives on mental illness by students from the Academy of Science and Entrepreneurship, and two collections of poetry, (*Dirty Birds* and *All of Our Lives*,) published for a retirement community where she worked and facilitated a poetry workshop.

Her work has appeared in *Chicken Soup for the Adopted Soul, Gyroscope Review, The Potomac Review, The RavensPerch, The Voices Project, and Veils, Halos and Shackles—International Poetry on the Oppression and Empowerment of Women* among other publications. Wells is a runner-up recipient of the Robert Frost Poetry Award in 2020. She is a frequent contributor to the Bloomington-based publication, *The Ryder*. Her memoir, *Dinner with Doppelgangers—A True Story of Madness and Recovery* was released in 2015.

Wells holds an MFA in Creative Writing from Spalding University, and an MA in English Literature from Butler University. She writes from Bloomington, Indiana.

www.ColleenWells.com.

www.ingramcontent.com/pod-product-compliance
Lightning Source LLC
LaVergne TN
LVHW090117080426
835507LV00040B/1046